DRIBBLE

A Poem

JACOB SMULLYAN

© 2015 by Jacob Smullyan
Book design © 2015 by Sagging Meniscus Press

All Rights Reserved.

Printed in the United States of America.
Set in Adobe Garamond with LaTeX.
Cover design by Anne Marie Hantho.

ISBN: 978-0-9861445-3-0 (paperback)
ISBN: 978-1-944697-10-5 (ebook)

Sagging Meniscus Press
web: http://www.saggingmeniscus.com/
email: info@saggingmeniscus.com

Contents

Preface · *v*
Dribble · *1*
Index of First Lines · *147*

Preface

In late summer and early autumn, 1983, when this work was composed, I was a disaffected Yale undergraduate with antisocial and artistic leanings, with no great love for the plutocratic atmosphere of my collegiate environs, and with no shortage of a smug arrogance as obscene as anything I deplored from my perch of adolescent superiority. An advantage of delusions which cut one off from the world, however, is that in isolation, strange dialects of creativity may form. *Dribble* is an example of a poetic artifact that certainly could not have formed in dialogue with anyone else's expectations. Standing in an impossible place, and committing fundamental errors without stint, it nonetheless succeeds at being itself. Often we have reason to be prouder of our original mistakes than our conventional successes, but failing to recognize it, disown ourselves. I am glad to have erred doubly: thirty years ago and more, by writing *Dribble*, and today, by acknowledging it.

Jacob Smullyan
June, 2015

DRIBBLE

I

Dribble. Whatsoever unceasingly, current fish. No submerged statuary hath prominence among ye. Green luxuries grapple frondulent candles and walk off perturbed, their digits scorched, their foreheads bent by the age-old light.

II

Mystery fowl alight upon
massive eternities feigning
myopia. No talons can
touch through the subtle skin of Death!
I lick it, unmoved. Some
membrane, an ominous incantation,
rustles under my tongue;
and I resort to unscalded cocoa.

III

A solar concentration inhabits my kitchen,
frowning on kettles with brilliance
as if to bake metal like meat,
like acts of creation unsustained. I spill.
No tremor shakes the floor; no tiles
beguile their linoleum and froth blackberry.
The old student with his spouse's frock
found nitro's advent with his arse up-aired.
Raise not the dark side to the sun.

IV

There is a green dust of this planet
far from the moon's green cheese;
there is a species of rot we cannot reach
though we sweep with drooping members,
mustachioed retirees of old, useless battles.
Methinks some brand of bug might scamper through,
a translucent purplish beetle in fey attire, hawking,
"I am the beast; grab an oar." And in his rags
his dirty smile.

V

The corner of the mouth
is a wall-eyed spider, whose
gaze droops off-color and dim
through tissues of frozen piss.
The Eskimo relieves himself to die,
impaled on the spear of his effluence;
and still-warm residues of smooches, oaths, and lies
spread a cobwebbed hammock from ear to ear.

VI

An origin is filth aground, a turd between lovers. In sleep they wobble apart, tired tops, and bouncing brains fart forth early morning deliveries. The truck. How do they know what they may carry, between their axles?

VII

Portentous, unread Talmud, on the high
shelf, untouched since Alkan. This space
I suspect tensegritous; this bulk
a gesture for the fragility of my skull;
this light, the hatred of the setting sun.
Does the scholar laugh when dead priests
vomit seed into his open dusk's window,
their billowing corpses exposed and enlarged,
their jaws wrapped with miraculous newspaper?
Or does he reach into some recess for an acorn
prophylactery, only to pluck forth a recondite balloon?
His eyeballs sag like Camembert until the final
drop is extinguished.

VIII

Curled horns of amber 'fore
a gnarled glimmer kneel and
bask their toesies, sudding.
Great barks of ambergris pace
on borrowed legs, their attenuate limbs
shorn from grasshoppers hanging
adherent to their sunken temples.

IX

Men bent at gloaming over their sandwiches,
their hand wenches. Leafy parks keep eyes
in back, beneath fronds of shame. The workmen
rise infertile for the homesome honeybuns,
the laundresses.

X

Hideous! The blossoms,
bloated by the breath of arthropods,
congregate near shrivelled
sprinters' legs, their teats
dug deep into soiled green blankets,
stretching away with sore red tongues
from the fangs which ensnare them.

XI

Sun-candles unfixed, in swarms
like aluminum scrap, begloomed
by lurid labels. A twilit
flicker, an open invitation
or a gratuitous confine;
a red-horned finger turned up
to the sun's deserted throne.

XII

Between sheaths of sightless grasses
squats most of a rabbit, silent
for dread. A tan archway leads
past tender halitosis to
mama's marination. Here,
stewed with thistle, locust,
carrot, and grasshopper,
a horsefly crawls in its ear.
Its immobile globes are halved;
pearly ringlets to grace
piratical physiognomies.

XIII

Jelly and ritual; the syllable
hopping like whiskers on the asthmatic
wheeze of methylated spirit,
the retiring gaze of a codfish.
Life on a plate. The great old men
in aspic, my fork, tantalized
like spaghetti, shies away from
the altar of its imprecations.

XIV

A crystal glass of sputum
is refrigerated, to pour lead
over dredged sea life. The
connoisseur's whoreson takes
the mards from his mouth,
scraping his teeth
with bubos like sandpaper.
Down the narrow paths
through his father's nose
rolls a fossilized ṣkull
from the kitchen floor
of a Japanese restaurant;
between his nostrils, an
immobile flank of cannons
and bowling balls, stacked tight
against sneezes and the light green fluids
who have frothed there.

XV

A midget iguana crawls back to sea,
to emulate the smoking mounds
of blubber, pure or malign, who
romanticize the horizon. Along
stony banks he swims until his elder's rock.
In fright his tail, a humiliate rudder,
clings like lichen, like moss to Rotunda;
naught resembles it more than a snared, canned sardine.

XVI

Beneath the rapids in suspension
within an aerated ooze are
heavy bubbles, sores of deuterious air,
and trout like cutlasses.
Through their snouts they curdle
the marmalade, spewing out
a hopeless residue behind their gills,
a weighty dripping overflow like
a bunch of white grapes.

XVII

Heady wombs approach the ravine,
snorting sooty incense, possessed
by galvanized sunglasses. Upon
his head a triangular protractor
is glued, a Stetson in the clouds
perpendicular to the red shift's cries.
The toupée is attached with a stake and
mallet to the breast of his eagle Ferrari.
Chip, chip. Like the sneeze in my dream,
the cabbie's outlet on the Verazzano,
his hot snot is hurled, suicidal eagerness for
life.

XVIII

The glare of twenty-six preens in inverse proportion
my dullish greenery where the rabbi drinks soda
and burps, constricting his lineage with burnt
hempen cords and long intervals. Bad for his eyes,
he constructs without effort a marmalade of
ambiotic aspic with cream cheese, a cervical
drunkenness where his touch has no priority
over magnetic repulsion, a receptable for
scorched retinas and wandering children.
Beneath his eyes hang two jellyfish,
squirming in tiny nets; when the chiropractor
tugs on his spine they are pulled up to his ducts
and vanish hungrily into his skull. It is then
that he begins to type.

XIX

The tinned sardine is a headless whore,
whose innards nourish through spitting.
Robert's sandwich bristles with tails;
his bench reeks of oil and gluttony.
Unconsumed, upon a towel he drops a leftover,
and torches his brains in the wind.

XX

A vast chart hangs from a purple clotted cloud
unable to dissipate, a pressurized boil with its
flag unfurled, its trumpet cauterized by figures.
In weeny processed print the message reads:
"Interviews between seven and nine; grocery
from eight to ten; wounds from nine to eleven;
Oedipus at noon." You call the vet, he produces
black dirt from his sock and worse from his trousers;
when he explodes, a single drop of colored rain
falls to scald his rented car. Go home.

XXI

A crumbling binding upon a hill startles
the nestling raven, whose red extracted flesh
he offers meekly upon a found sacrarium.
Upon the text he drops from his beak a black
artery, pulled from his breast like a
parachute cord; with this, he has no
recourse but to burst in censorious flame
and fly yapping into the cave.

XXII

The color of scissors, scissors who
snip little folds of enraged flesh,
bleeds down the forehead, soaking
the dinner napkins. Men at the table
pocket their watches and glance
erectly at each other's postures,
their right hands encroaching upon
their neighbors' goblets. Beneath the presidium
crawls a masked mohel, furtively snatching
the garnish of State.

XXIII

A high harness rests on the hillside,
too mute to gnash its chrysanthemums
with richly deserved spores, sundried
roe, its skins hydraulically taut.
Robert lowers his hind upon the tubercle,
twisting his spine until its reads
Help Wanted in script. Around him
swim the bloated ova, vapid caviar blasted
from the pressurized depths, mocking vagrants
taunting the aspiring poacher, and a vast horse
charges forth, bony yet inspired, crushing
and mangling what fundaments are met.

XXIV

A soul is laid out for stew, configured
like chicken parts. The task of the cook –
to bury his snout into the underwing and
soil his teeth with feathery floss –
is my green archaic fish, dimly descried
as indentation on the plastic rear panel
of a leased refrigerator. With every fading hour
some rib of this shoots its pate and another
shred of scrawn confounds my crucial choice.

XXV

At the secret signal the lizard-skinned forearm
sets out, growing fibers along its banks for
corporate reinvestment. With a nod I censure
its twitch, and autist fingers, the forgotten
residue of ancient prunings, start forth from the shadows
to slither across the tiles and be blinded
by mousetraps, G-forced scaffolding.

XXVI

The sun on the grass kneads forth prudish lumps
of tears, incandescent insects like wet kisses.
They roll on their shiny tanks, confident
of the ventilation of legs like nosehair
and the receding, sunken pools monsters
call their hearts. Hard nits flog the air,
scrapnel abounding for textural contentment,
pitiless knots provoking in meek, cellular flesh
a futile, painterly rage.

XXVII

Death is in squirrels or encased in what
even under blankets radiates a sickly green
reflection, the cold thick eyeglasses of
an ichthyologist along the roadway, shedding
hopeless pelts over the puddles of wastrels,
the jar where like a mythic hand-me-down
seedy round berries are jammed, no longer
self-contained, but an ether
for the damned and the needy,
a sweetened bile which the electrified
muscle accepts with sweating submission,
the gut's corrosive weeping.

XXVIII

White, grey, and green, the mucus of
long reflection is brought to trial,
escorted from its lair by men of conscience,
and led to the chamber of rumination,
whose discords pass as wisdom for those
who cannot taste the revelatory stools
whose bloody crapping overturns its justice.

XXIX

In the garden where feckless resins
coagulate beneath shadowy petals, the
bones of the eight children are enervated
of calcium, and the white schoolmarm's
chalky poker violates their medullae oblongatae
with a ticklish needle, risen red
like the secret eye. Pricked, the green brains
fold like Western towns, vivisected model students.

XXX

Noodles strung in shit reach
for my eyeballs, clamoring for
inviolate space in the sun. Repeatedly
I nail a palm to my forehead,
driven by a thirsty gale, but
faith in intrinsic values is
a depersonalized Olympian,
whose balls of fire like spotty turds
fall random and scorch the base
of divinity with persistent excrement,
the malign graffito of nature.

XXXI

The sun threatens my house, claiming
natural rights of force. Giving them
full credit I cannot respect them, and
with a classic green candle I thrust
tawdry smoke at the ozone, warping my
human demise with an encompassing death
in self-molesting flames.

XXXII

Gummed labels of another year
hang browning from recalcitrance,
a cloud of null statement. Silent,
Robert regards his arm, a torturous branch
like a fried noodle, member
of the lackadaisical, will-less
even to fulfill its apathy
in violent soy sauce.

XXXIII

Like a green path of air
hornets symbolize their minks,
casting fruitless vegetables upon
priests and their aspersions. Witches
subsist in bubbles, groping for
breathing room; in swarms a conflagration
of vital lungs crawls like an
academic germinate back
to the source, the stung furuncle
of the stage.

XXXIV

I cannot relate what feeds upon bodies,
chewing the forgotten cud of corpses
from their now gaping dry mouths; my glands
are splenetic like honeycombs, spongy
like the wrath of an abstraction. But
the wet depressions of their attentions
lie fetid about us like sunken lightships.

XXXV

The sun busies himself with another quarter,
and we escape notice, λανθάνομεν. Bereft
of sense we stumble, gore-eyed chaperones,
leaning on the upraised limbs of men
buried under the sun. We cauterize our brows
with lemon juice and coat our blood-gorged parts
with an ice-cream not even night keeps chill.
Above the hamper four dwarves tap the bowls of spoons
with unseen impatience.

XXXVI

Without wings the runner
flees his perch, fingering his cerebrum
with elongated toothpicks and pincers
lately palmed. The sweetmeat nestles
snugly within his hollow pawn and, the castle unfolded,
removed organs clog the streets,
a traffic in formaldehyde
thus obscuring the grounds of crosswords.

XXXVII

Rescinded like a man crossing the street,
glancing with anxiety at his spats,
the horse raises his lip like a stage curtain
for Toulouse-Lautrec, and drops into the
lap twenty white-legged dancing-girls,
plump, warm, and reeking of flesh,
twenty crumbs of pure incandescent manure
around our ankles.

XXXVIII

The prize is a hot towel, a
potato suffering iced intent
of pop-eyed hordes. A greenhorn in a bowler
becomes prominent for the ascetic
abacination of the nails on his abacus,
and heavy hands clapping lotion on his back
provoke the continental drifting we outside
his spectacles cannot note.

XXXIX

Like Robert to engage the arms of an octopus
for the only waltz. "*Gemeinheit!*" in repeated
notes, they respect no chair let from
the kangaroo shaft of a lorry. Bulging,
around the cityday they scourge, posting
stickers behind medicine cabinets and
inserting the bulbs of eye-droppers into
their throats to rival the epiglottis.

XL

Persistent turd, where three-legged
omnivores hop like ants, careening in circles
with cigars. Again and again two men await
a silence, suspended in an aerosol foam
that forever has shreds of wind.
One reaches forth Shelley coated with
almond pretzels and pestilent grass,
a smoke from the ranks guarded
by shoulders; the other, manipulating
his medulla oblongata by means of wires
and his fingers, embedded irremediably
in his nostrils, greets the floating nuts
with anger.

XLI

Robert, knowing snozzles, grins at artichokes,
his long membranous hands wildly scoured and wrapped,
tropical leaves, around a hydrant with red
chipped and vibrant paint. The municipality
like a housed screech engages
cogs and eggshells for purposes
of containment inside their sensuous
arteries of scalding fluids.

XLII

Hydra like florid dwarves
hold horses captive under sinks,
gritting their pusillanimous toes
with earwigs like spitting.
Horrid necks are those: peeling lettuce,
they accept a strident liberty,
and like flags of forgettable nations
they walk across streets, embassies
of embarrassment.

XLIII

A horde approached, carrying
soft-spoken silverware. Theodore
rose, dropping withered malariac
wombs like dried rattling gourds,
and opened his mouth, exposing
to appease hungry dark skins
the locusts who swarm over
his reddened epiglottis.

XLIV

Frozen green forces imbibe their livery,
casting dice through crystal nightshade
into brokenjawed craws, who like
unthinking oysters shell eyes and
locomote by theorized flatus.
Snorting wisdom, the gelatine relents,
a heaving glacier plopping blue scoops of melon sherbet
into the briny punch.

XLV

A practising surgeon, his glasses affixed to a whiskified Polaris
but his gaze like a casual vehicle from Turin mass transit
blinking palely forwards, loses his son in a wet towel,
whose sticky message he rereads before it disappears:
the holy impression of a lewdly mustachioed hoaxster
shrouded impishly; a veiled obelisk.

XLVI

Robert sucks diamonds for retreating whores
whose gums revoke license and obtain green
satisfaction, a bubbling sore to sear the ridicule
of no man's grub. Behind his spine a tingling doorknob
is sold for a teacup of white glue.

XLVII

Seven deaths walk the streets
sodomizing themselves on the ghosts
of gas-lamps. Four men in raincoats
cluster around the dim light, and
the violin creeps along the wet street
under awnings with earrings.

XLVIII

Dried Zoroastrians cry aloud to the sandwich-maker,
requesting Polish mustard. In their valley
they feast on soft things, their five thousand worth
of generation, and they pack away where no one
may see the unsightly cuneiform ambitions
which show a thirst for blood and then,
cradled in peace, fall asleep with a drop
of milk in their mouth's corner, smiling
without eyes.

XLIX

Torrid waists are encircled
by brass foaming glazed caviar
over the one burble of the flawless skin,
the ὀμφαλός. No wiggling exterminates
the wily ants, who at the shot
teem like blood from her nostrils
and consume her with fiery stings.

L

The doctor's visor casts a shadow
over the medullae of a cadaver,
the skin peeled back like a pink blanket
to expose the necking and nestling
of hearts and oranges, lungs bladders and spleens,
kidneys, testes, and fruitless broods of ova,
all pinned back and manacled from contact
in the doctor's blackness where
with brass-toned certitude they turn
irresistably blind and greyly stone-dead.

LI

Your mouth drops a thread,
a chink of drowsiness to extirpate
horrid roses, orchids with pink
underdone wings shorn from fledermice
in the midst of sightless hooting flight.
A black space among your teeth
is a knight, darkly mantled, his visage
impaired but his lance unerring
like an ungiggled kiss, but from the mass
will arise a neighbor; the overwhelming crowd
perfects a grin and swallows empty crowns,
sewn like buttons into the ulcered duodenum.

LII

Under the horizon there swoops a great bird,
master of gritted articles, spendthrift
of aerobic wrinkles, drowner of shopping fish,
carrier of capes and jutty-rocks, a black figure
sketched on pavement with appropriated chalk. With
no cry he sinks, giving off no light,
but submitting to an orange glow
where the sun submits to night.

LIII

At maximum carrot peelings, at the most
intense dredgings, the highest on high
gloried flotation, the asymmetrical ball of shit
riding the crest! The hero wears a hat
and a collar, the lariat by his side
swinging in the gale and dragging
impairingly in the turgid brown waters.

LIV

Greeting the hilarity of the gorgon
he increases his abdomen with wind
and swells his pockets by gathering
chestnuts. Like a black bird he
ascends, making the sky green,
in every repetition a virgin moment
and a fallen pellet, a mad seed
rejoining the fertile humus from
the warlock's pocket.

LV

Frigged eyes point outwards
at the sullen fish by ecstasy
unimpressed; thus with eager pity
I close them with fluid lips,
fervently forgetting, helpless blasphemers,
self-damned until they too
return pursed and gulping to the sea.

LVI

Quiescent rivers enlarge their troughs,
squeezing a white particulate angel-foam
in hominal emulation, with touching gropes
towards drooping willow boughs. The eyebrows of rocks
grate their drapes, shredding a rented
formal to bare their active strength
in silent, rapid immobility.

LVII

Silent forests respect mosses
which grope, spraying mesmerized
stones from the bladders of saints
and raising thin ankles, set deep
in rock, to squirt from their xylem
a dilute green lymph. Boots of children
snare the nestling of hanging boulders,
and a turfy mudslide snarls the streets,
where veiled shoes aspire to knees
on thin, so thin womanly legs.

LVIII

Forty are arranged. In cupboardlike
rows, the faces run with snot, noses
burst like cap-guns, spoiling the medallions.
Something sparked by a droplet of dew
chooses to arise despite its strict
confine, and the gunman's freedom,
trampled, becomes the exuberance
of a mongrel.

LIX

Like a gross formula embedded in
a juvenile dessert, a cactus
sweats a hearty amber and builds
itself a translucent cocoon with
a minaret like a Swedish ice cream cone. To this stickum
a firefly is affixed, counting its final
sparks of romance though every member's
knee-mired in the glue.

LX

Stormy dungeons rape the oarlocks,
giving flesh to watery mermaids
beneath a sheath of grapes and
denatured brandy, frozen like
a bed of ice, a pillow for
Hephaestus and willful Aphrodite,
smoking cigars through her ample
nostrils. He pins to her breastskin
a bronze he smithed, a martial medallion,
and his black tongue eagerly licks
the smoking blood, draining over her belly
between her legs, branding her folds
like a hot iron.

LXI

Behind the curtain of red steam, if
it is rent, appears a cauterized ghost,
lingering malignantly in the place of its
remission. It tootles a white-hot
arse-flute, and the notes spout succor
like a tossed purse of grapes, gristle
which engineers the erect charger.

LXII

Digging a wet hole in the mold
he finds the open eyes of gorgon,
the holy exhalation which electrifies
her weedy croplocks and lends them
venomous hearts, the clarity of her bent,
distracted brow, the delicious chinks
of her cracked-through gaze. He stares,
he loves; and Robert, fingering the knob
in his pocket, cannot budge it.

LXIII

Full of the granulate force of his grinder,
he walks, nauseated, along celerous banks
where two flutes in cases have been confused
with a gentleman's umbrella. A quarrel
behind his back emerges to insert a microscopic
Kügel in the small of his hind, a drilled speck
of dust, a billiard bearing fickle fission
smithed close to his patriotism, and a sublime
pain like chocolate and Ferris wheels, a panging
vertiginous love sickening the gut, comes intently
from the corner of the room and overwhelms
him without any fuss.

LXIV

Warped bridges sort their toiletries,
fogging their muskets with spurts of
white fire where the cords, luminous,
drape through clouds of ground eyewhites.
Looming over the coiled ropes, wheels
within wheels, a Mercedes spurns its
caravan of doors, and sheds with
the impudence of Houdini its fenders,
a wilting butterfly.

LXV

Froh-ed Horace is the pastoral wench,
making chow from depucelated chickpeas.
Humming a rondeau, she clenches two fingers
and pulverizes a boil, releasing
an acidic serene, a sacred vapor
inspiring in its angered blue plasma
a cosmic religiosity, an oceanic
embrace.

LXVI

Seated frogs introduce smoke
through embryonic channels to
a network of broken glass and
hot-shot tubes. Hopping between
flaccid, forsaken rabbit-ears,
they poplessly bulge, murmuring
chrysalides, Yorkshire puddings
immersed in chlorophyll, and
mockingly extend ashen tongues,
astonishing short circuits.

LXVII

Dissident hazes engulf roving vermin,
who weave across streets en masse in the rain.
The roads by thirty degrees tilt over,
raising the dungeons obliquely within sight
and within the range of ravaging teeth
when the mist must muffle all cries.

LXVIII

A dearth of overhanging toruses or spindles,
cresting freckled folds of dishwater in which
to immerse the humorous handles, bright-eyed
physiognomy of the faceless faculties, or
the crapulent force-feeding of the fickle
pulleys, an apparatus self-sustained, existing
to shut itself down, molds in white mud
a twisting doughnut with sockets for eyes,
as if in expectation within of an arising soul.
A committee is formed of bloodshot raincoats,
standing about with cigarettes and indifferent yo-yos
around the casted thing while vinegar rains blue
on their heads, sullenly corrosive for the sake of hope.

LXIX

An acid swarms on the floor, grinning foci in search of manilla. Plump feet present their toes, nails dessicated by diverted care, and a phoenix walks by in his winter suit.

LXX

Fortuitous morticians spit out gristly tears
through their guffaws as they soften the corpse
in their saliva-sapped mouths. Their toothless gums
clamp down on reconstituted fingers, their enzymes
prepare the flesh for persnickety connoisseurs,
the rich man's maggots; the saline juice from the ducts,
some oceanic vestige, preserves the jacket and tie
for eventual reincarnation.

LXXI

A ripe jug of gilded flies
tinkles on the mantle, sorting
dugs and printed mantras
into neat games with cherry tomatoes,
an organic children's pastime.
From the erupting earth beneath the niece
springs a camouflaged missile, bearing
vats of transfused blood and fishdew
dredged from a buried sea.

LXXII

Cutlets provide the hostelry for green molds,
small gizzards straining for Georgian rocks.
Headless they lie upon platters, reciting
Celtic myth and establishing parallels with
the aching *Kopf*, striving to engulf a long-roasted
apple by inserting its grappling-hook into
the furniture of horticulture, challenged
for diamonds and the earthy mounds pierced
by magma-driven roots. Like a trestle the
rock is clambered upon with a gay silence,
the quiet of a clinging moss, of an orange sauce
congealed to an aspic.

LXXIII

I am presented upon the occasion
with the liver of a mutual friend,
shorn from his corpus by immutable beaks
and gilded for mantlepieces and too light
cases for books. The donor pulls back my head
by the hair, and forces the organ on my nose,
smothering me, blinding me with allied juices
which drip loudly, incessantly from lofty
stalactites into my bloodshot, blackened eye;
and my heart-compelled mouth, panting open wide,
like a gutter accepts the turdous bile
that oozes from the sleeve of my thoughtful,
solicitous companion.

LXXIV

Greeted by the headlights at gloaming,
I raised my arm in crossing and persisted,
incrementally vanishing into my brown winter suit.
At once, while the driver lowered his eyes
to scrutinize fresh-picked nasal slough,
my trousers shat through me and my divers
segments, all in accord, became one streak
of chocolate pudding. Like a chicken neck,
the imaginary exile, cast away from Alexandria,
was pilloried and squashed in his self-determined home.

LXXV

Fertile imps fret over turnips, counting
crops with pointed scythes and debating
subterrestrial currents. A fish is found,
half mown in the turf; and the thirsty landlord
falls to the plough, chawing the odiferous outcasting
of his faery tenants.

LXXVI

Wimped digits flick their fronds,
exhorting wombats to empty their pockets
and spill their beans on the mountain-tops,
where fish of old frollicked among
the feathered bears, grinding basted fronts
near the lavaflow and the latrine. Holding
with the utmost gravity the heavy smile
in his hand, the forehead folds, the cards
scatter, and the mouth drops to shatter
on the mattress, where a thread of dew
leads to a once beloved pair of lips.

LXXVII

Short-haired, among the cilia which and cilia
she becomes every day, the greenhouse domestic, hard-skinned,
a slipper-shaped arthropod holding the husk
and waving flakes of legs. Foreign to dimpled
musks, she fawns the dire, the grotty snorts,
and with a handful of menstrual snot
she approaches Israel, a Herzl bearing sand
smiling confidently.

LXXVIII

Seven doorknobs are confounded, and knocks
like dry wheezing coughs fall into the
absorbent blanket of sound, emerging naked
like uncovered adulterers. Who's there.
With each dismal reminder, Robert's blood
rushes to the head, palpable proof of his
guilt and his audacity; and the passages
reclose upon his stammering silence,
 walls upon which to splinter all things' head.

LXXIX

A corridor, humid with the panting
of a hungry dog, a bloodthirsty poodle,
an anarchist waving his tail no longer
from glee but to publicize the patches
made bald by neighborly teeth, suddenly
darkens; as though night had come, or
a time of forgiveness. But inside the black missile
come running white shapes, billowing like dim sheets
with tails, dragging frisky white ropes
to bind at last a heated animal.

LXXX

Fidgeting with overgrown moats, broken
asunder and reglued with off-white ice,
a clotted cream of a consistency martyred
by the winged asparagus burbles up from
unseen cracks, flying darkly to dim the sky
of bright tossed oranges, gold catching
the buttery sun. The huskyblack witch,
shorn of all tinder, floats out her window
an umbrella, sailing down away on a flood
of coffee beans Camelot's nocturnal
horsehaired throne to a silken blot,
a spreading spill of India ink on the curtains
of the horizon.

LXXXI

Drinking lemonade, the forests give
deep content to borrowed gates, salvaging
sparrows and the kin of faucets suckled
by once spewn mortar. The woods, fogging
the mustard of the evening, shampoo their treetops
and dip branches in a bubbly foam,
an historical plasm emulsified with bristles,
to scour the camouflaged bark-flies
and bare their dry tongues, their rain-retentive
leaf, for manna-Godpiss.

LXXXII

Many codfish coerced the hound, tearing
straps and colored buttons to release
the bursting earnest, which fugitively
dashes from the gate, surrendering its eyes,
a red-hot pointer in the alien wind.
Diving the depths, it drags along empires,
plunging a mind like an angered coal
through deep-delved hollow roads into obsessing,
darksome, head-pounding flight.

LXXXIII

Gripping figged masses, the head bears down
and gorges the cords of cerebration (by agreement
lids closed) so that their metamorphosis into
fresh-scooped green cocoons, squirming with
reddish dumb life, cannot escape the enraged
mucal cavities whose imprisoning walls are
shredded and bled by scrawny, petty fingernails.
Inside now is the presence of another; and yet
more real to his self are the groping, striking rebels
of his eyes.

LXXXIV

Gyped envoys fork the harpooned kites,
wearing no skins of scaly creatures but
carrying in black medical satchels
the corroded teeth of glaring birds,
whose flight in the upper strata was
interrupted by a big-armed god, an
assured bear with rending claws and
pincers from the dentist's tray. The sullen messengers
coil their rope and examine the necklace of trinkets,
half dissolved in mammary blood dried with acid
on the sharpened enamel of the sky.

LXXXV

A belt of cutting crystal lies
blankly underfoot, collecting a puddle
of scrapings and rotting pears,
the juice of discarded tobaccy. Singling
One, it reforms the sunrays, capturing
their ethic inside a talismanic pyramid
and farting with leaden purity a flame
to relight a spent, peaten fag.

LXXXVI

Dealing with gaunt, spoken wits,
he shakes hands and feels their digits
dislodge in his paw like the crumbling children
of nightshades. Grimacing and thrusting his beak
into the ether, the candidate returns grey,
approaching himself to congratulate, estranged
and newly foolish, a visitor in his own mind.

LXXXVII

Like a particolored rope his mind wheedles its length,
rolling around its intrinsic whoredom for the disreputable gain
of thought. A certain space, a synaptic revulsion, protects
his nerve-shorn sense; his red-scoured brain, inflamed
by his own strangling self-invasion to conquer his toes,
a swimming ambition in solidifying lemon-flavored waters,
must squirt out its grapes, thus giving rise
to the translucent ruse of neighborly wine.

LXXXVIII

Pustules like wire fret their tongs,
spicing pickles with dandified whispers
and crinkle-cut fortified wounds. No entrance
is permitted for gawking crones, storks
whose bony legs are out of joint, disfigured
by bandaged loads of aces and queens,
flippered scores of hindering. For freedom
the feathered mouth dreebs. Fimpled gispers
nick the fonts, striding their pens into
new, unblemished barrels; stronger dimples
blossom with red forges, kniding fins
with gouged quippers. Hwab.

LXXXIX

Fipply nisps fint the dampers
greasing discared cords with noisome
nickel. Haughtily the chrislike
knoiks emerge, alongside doughty Jerry
fingering the forty fought latitudes
with intemperate impertinence.

XC

Greasy Bobby fits the bill, smelling
of remaindered fish-chips, mounting
on the disused verbs. With spines
he lashes the spar in the gale,
tying the flag of hope in despair
with slipping, crumbling vertebrae,
cooling its friction with white vaseline,
an ode to a wet death.

XCI

Dimly licks assault the inkwell, grinning
for the ambassador to fifty stakes behind
the van where the maid airs his peruke.
The paleface drains his scalp of red droplets
while faintly from his pate there bursts a whalelike
snort of white, a coroner's sheet to conceal
the coupled misdemeanor.

XCII

Naughty fibs cannot sort their whites,
but laugh at their drawers, unopened,
submerged in jaundiced tears. They are
nasty not, the gaudy prints with which
their rounds are swathed, but the fruitless
juice of distant inks, a Sanskrit sandhi,
a measureless rule with a sharp cutting edge
the tailor, blind servant of your fate, wraps
around your scrappy red neck.

XCIII

Tusked mailmen ride to work, hanging
their keychains from their nostrils. Their
route, like a cask of cave-set Spain wine,
is the dodging of calcified icicles, the
revulsion of the ivory-strangled octopus,
the shrouded mockery of the colorless wine-tap
hanging to deceive like explosive batons, a cynic's
letter-bombs drained of impulse.

XCIV

Gaping at the filtered star, natives
in mini-skirts dance the challah,
tossing fresh risen loaves into a black,
unforgiving light where some receptacle, a frigid
Eskimo goddess and her poachy, halfscratched salmon,
awaits the hot poppyseed with disavowing breath.

XCV

Claws of lobsters form ridges
upon the miniscule larvae there hatched,
tubular ecstasies waving stained hairs.
But their half-closed eyes betray
an inborn malcontent, some fishiness
whose evanescence sharp stately clippers
with detachment early snap.

XCVI

The bout, like diffident brands,
seethes and excavates thoughty fish.
Guilty breathers, the tired old man
with the snarls of youth embraces them
with enzymatic tonsils, knowing their bones
as he knows his own.

XCVII

A substantial plasma, self-reflecting,
emanates like lifesavers sinking in
an empty sea, a screen with rusty knobs,
its glassy surface marred and nicked.
A ravishing lock, shoulders tensed, consumed,
afire with intent stars, thinks nothing,
until open and torched by a peaceful indifference
it regains pleasure, only to find it burgled.

XCVIII

Kaspar, inspecting an apple, deems it *klug*, with enthusiastic attribution embracing its soul and eating the world calmly, his mouth full of death. Crawling about the cavern in which white tombs are lain to lean two-storied where the dark is full, green burbles, ridiculed moles, squirm unseen, gangrenous putterings whose homeland is pure.

XCIX

A sublime crusade is planned for pilgrims, a surefooted
sympathetics for childish figures grappling
like red-faced wrestlers in the wanderlusty sand.
Suctioned cheeks are present too, shorn enormous
and twitching in the grass, bloody red chunks
of stratified blubber. Heaving these onto camels,
the babes pander their flocks, out striking to
wrap the unpossessing bards with ladylike sheets
which conceal strangers from their poverty.

C

Lotus crap drips grease onto the snozzled
fries, ducking midgets into stillborn, sophisticated
lords, highbrowing with the deep. Horticultured
owls do not flap, but perched disdainfully
they sleep at night and during the day
shoot contemptuous pellets of sanitary,
oft-indulged egesta. Rare buds, they
prune their wisdom, fertilizing their doctrines
with aluminum scrap and steaming alkaloids.

CI

Disregarded hoots resound in the mist
which like a dreamer's forest settles
all around and wraps one tight like a
truer skin until breathlessly one wakes.
A man out hunting is discerned, with
feathers in his cap; he falls to his knee
as if harkening to a woeful cry,
a shriving scream of pity that sears him through.
Now palely he is gone, by himself posted
away, delivering the message we did not hear
which even our rent hearts cared not to sense.

CII

With blood goes pallidly
a stranger, sheetfaced, dragging along ropes
behind his mutely chawing horse,
who spits at times a brittle thread
like curt tobacco. This ghost
like men eats flesh, while rivulets
of gore show up distinctly red on
the one white tatter he's lent his steed
to suck; passionless he comes
to men in fever, a leech, swift
yet transfixed, an obliging old companion
and aid to ancient desperados
with whom he shares a tameless mare.

CIII

Dorsal fins are found afloat,
compounded with half-eaten clam dip.
Yellow seeds and memorable poppies
seek Robert out, sedulously waving
stumpy fish.

CIV

Frozen ozones greet their wimps,
spindling factors of haughty self-abuse
over long reams of nickel-plated hornet-nests.
Gored dessicators dissect their perinea,
discovering coal-blacked, oil-clogged capillaries
and basted rackets, well-lathed crackpots.

CV

Steamed rotors nudge the naughty nuggets,
coating with steel the soft-hearted turds
now ground, imps floating in tomato sauce,
to a rasty pulp, ejecting sprays of juniper
and discontinuous fumes, coyly rising.
Hawks cough despondently upon the blue plates,
and their talons on the high-chairs
bulge, developing felt wrappers.

CVI

Anxious dogs flick the outcast cans,
leading robots to the den of the pariahs.
In the caravan, dwelling as a gold-shorn
mole, a cavern resounding the bladdered ghoul
trots uncertainly around the glutton on
fretful wooden spokes, precisely treading
on scream-stuffed tails whose bursts
evoke metallic uproars, vectoral dins
piercing drums and heaving aluminum
for half-starved goats.

CVII

Daughters sense the necks of minions
sinking complacently into their breasts,
bridges laden with explosive chocolates,
sharply mocked immersed cashews for
a soul's appeasing embrace while one stares
alone at the bright celestial cigars.

CVIII

Gaskets blaze a rancid fume,
a stinging empty eye aflame
amidst enamel. The bent, indifferent
hose, black beneath the succoring sun,
makes sullen piecemeal of the pulp,
shredding the inperforate pupil
for the sake of fluid vision,
a clean tearlike motive. The tatters,
dripping sponges of honey, endure
a ragged wipe, and clack! by
a concealing license plate
the hungry torch is spent.

CIX

Decent members at the spittoons
converse loudly in splats, knocking
friends' optic bulbs smartly
with wads of corrosive secretion.
The enzymatic gospel like a piece of smut
is told; circulating chummy gobs
the keepers of the faith
sweep out the ruddy sockets
where private gods had squat,
blots lusting for excision.

CX

Greasing the fender, the youth turns around,
flashing horizontal stripes, orange ways
impersonating thinness. His toothy jaw ajar,
in his hand the cake of creamy butter, he seeks
his pappy tongue; smiling he reaches in and finds
the floundering fish. The root-yanked cold cut
spreads new lard upon the lavish, sun-reflecting car;
and behind the wheel the eager boy displays
his new spacious grin to the freshly painted highway
on the stretch where one may not pass.

CXI

The tortoise rigorously proceeds a step
before toppling the wavering boulder
to fall and smash its shell.
Soft mallowy plates cave under
like milk-enervated toast
oppressed by mindless slabs of butter.
The grunting grey head squints and affirms
the pinkly touch-sore skin
whose rupturous membranes loose
a cherry-red magma oozing swiftly up
through the quaking shards of armor.

CXII

Dishtowels, smoking a fibrous batch of green larvae,
swirl vibrantly in luxurious sweat
trepanning miniscule droplets of fricative filth
with scourging turds, meteors of oft-soaped skins.
The diving hands are nailed by brushless, stroking
    streams of heat
from the white sands imparted, uncolored mirrors
bequesting an unspoken eloquence of spectacle,
a still rocket on a fiery jet.

CXIII

Like a bratsome wok, splitting
complacent cucumbers and presenting
scalded oil humbly, a bomb in the mail,
beneath his lumbering armor
two eyes and a lance are stored,
the eagle's skill and the blood-tipped blunter.
For dinner he foils tall leaves, quoiting
their tender phloem; a threat to
shrubs, he quaffs chlorophyll,
staining his lips with green life
in anticipation of lurid satisfactions.

CXIV

A buzz like a white sheet
is the tetany of the tongue,
an inperforate throbbing sheath
approaching constant fire.
With minute, procrastinating slits
the organ is slivered,
and white almonds in abundance
dance, released from the orifice
like long-suppressed cries,
an overflow of white from red,
an idealization of the sun.

CXV

Fibbed snorters cower now,
their faces, red and bloated,
become swollen capitals for
toppled columns, fallen arches.
In the corner they crouch, collected,
the works of trust and delirious calm.

CXVI

Slyly hugging the enclosure, Robert returns,
an ashplant swinging from the bridge of his sunglasses.
Dishes float on irises, golfing eyeballs
and polishing their red glaze with chamois.
Robert confounds the rags, brutally
fishing them from their suds, howling
as he wrings them dry.

CXVII

Tonight the moon is a polite reflective platter,
a fresh-washed porcelain squeaking in isolation
whose old fish-bones and untouched asparagus
have fallen, exuding no light,
through black billions of miles
to Earth, meteors unannounced.
A farmer in contemplative pause
while a horse busies his ass
sees the limp overcooked vegetable
crash down like sequoia from the sky;
with practical wonderlessness
he plows in the blob, feeding his soil
with unnatural gifts.

CXVIII

Sinking into the white porcelain quagmire,
Robert, smiling impishly beneath new-found dark lenses,
discards his poker, his flushed contraption,
and bidding adieu tangles his toes
in an unknown mesh of copper roots.
With a gurgling, triumphant cry
he's gone; behind he's left
the monkey-twisted stick, the leaning
glazed branch, panting mutely
against a silver-coated doorknob
seductively closed.

CXIX

Under the dark city the tunnel runs,
an obsessed vehicle for billiard balls,
rocks removed and rolling
in narrow tracks, stout snowballs
squeezing past the banks of valleys.
The bilious sludge burbles, suffused
with slime; in changeless motion
as slow as saccharine the honeydew
surges up through worsted pockets.

CXX

A subversion of grasses spills wine
on the cocktail napkins, seeping through to
the vinyl quartet. Limp strings result
in public strangulations, suicides
performed by experts.

CXXI

A cat, sprung from Deutschland,
comments on the grasshopper
in my trousers. Haunting lawns
are disarmed by a kaleidoscope
on a winning folding chair, but the
spoon-eyed inhabitants perch on their
swollen victims with temerous impunity.

CXXII

Whips lie clear on lutulent sagas,
limpid vermicelli granted alchemical potency
over the sauce. Smattering teeths, blind
to the cloud, smack with gay serenity
beneath the latent cumulate coils
realizing unthought welts.

CXXIII

Forgotten physicists fondle babes,
pulling forth crevices recondite
from knobs for perennial pinball, springs
from which corroded bearings,
swirling blackly about us like
burning shrapnel, scarring snot,
must inexorably pour.

CXXIV

Squalidly waiting, dangling from a seated finger
my wasted can, I fold the tents,
grappling torrid hooks and curvaceous
knives fast pulled like frozen roses.
In the park, between petals of rusted
flowers, orange soot scrubbed between
my toes, the lastsupper-aged Semite
smiles to recite his Torah,
and in the green lawn my spikes
have tearfully been thrust,
the last wrenching stabs of an abandoned litterbug.

CXXV

From his vest at the bus-stop,
where the girl nearby pats her necklace
with a distant fern plucked from
dyed roots, a vat is produced,
charred and ridden with black biting heroes,
equations swathed in rider's boots
bearing the jaws of fierce tautology.
He evinces to her smoking eyes
holy bloodshots, a sentimental baking dish,
the old familiar glassware, goggly thick,
refractive, holding within the oven-fresh
ice-cream a burbling tawny soup
all slicked over by the heavy men
at the overshining twilight when with
a pool cue he screws up
his bulging red eyes.

CXXVI

Spatulas snicker behind the fronds,
waving their rubber heads like
inchoate wristwatches, ticking
forests spewing regular tributaries
from the masked mounts to the
splashful faucets which obscure time
and faint, desperate pleas.

CXXVII

Rolling dander incinerates the court,
falling fibers and erecting orange
sunflowers. The vacancy of a cracked,
pleasantly mad old clock haunts the bairn,
lying awake to catch the humming, feeble wheeze
which chimes a brave and throaty midnight
when the sun glances off the ancient, smiling petals.

CXXVIII

The cat sleeps, while rubber burns
elsewhere. Dealt houses express
their cards, flushing panes and
madly heaving spades from the roof.
The senior lion yawns, lighting
habitual icons with his yellow tail.

CXXIX

The mustachioed Deutscher peels away leaves,
finding sebacious globules, mardous stomata
gurgling like urgent flutes, the erect throats
of featherless waifs, with radarous trumpets
hauling in the aboriginal seed; potential potency,
strength in helplessness. But the gizzards
are crunching are turds, at anti-historic revuliments
teeming with crimes, the sane triumphs, the
illicit revocations and shining conquests
of the weak. The fronds are ingermane,
subverted dice crumbling like tortuous monoliths,
leaders distributed to the distaste of microbes.
With hot wax, a vain white ardor, unser Herr
locks his cilia in a daylong staunch embrace;
the paramecia perish on his starchy face.

CXXX

In the wok sounds a bell,
a buzzer tracing a parabola
like a shell-shocked stumbler's
spit, blasted uneven and frozen
along the sides of a bowl.
The scalding greens are introduced,
bowing to the browning heat;
dried in towels, they bathe in oil
near the spice-encased tendons,
sinews disengaged and membranes untapestried,
to cloak the modest deaths and
starkly bare the exposed life,
streaming its gravy through the thousand hungry gutters,
cisterns of our life-blood
deep-cored in the vitals of our loves,
from whence a methanous portent belches,
reeking of sizzling black mushrooms.

CXXXI

A gasp, a gurgle through the clogged gelatine
which enlists the purple luxury of our synapse,
imports a rare fragility to the crux,
a green bubble of the East, an originating spore
caught in the very execution of its essence.
The weighty gentleman admires its filmy coat,
the grime of space travel, and with tweezers
refines a fur, a hairy sheath to decorate,
to obscure and harden the precious ethers
for playing bounce-the-ball inside the Quad,
for sending it the way of grace, the mutable
changed immutable, decreed from pulpits
with spite for remembrance, from desk-seated
officialdom on the comfy cushion of Romance.
The death rattle of the man in a bowler
is imbued by time, by the holy moment
when all doctrines come to naught.

CXXXII

Fists cannot clap, and the robbers,
smiling appreciatively through
their stockings, drop their bundles
to free their arms. Crisp melbas
sing in the oven, losing steam
through hard whistles. Underneath
the jam is a crunchy aliment
seeking ears, a blessing
from Nabisco. The action
of the whole being defined
behind the shower curtain
as the inactions of the many,
no knuckles spare their blood,
and the premier scrounges
for laurels among the afterbirths,
shkotzim pandering to shlemiels.

CXXXIII

The nuisance is an aggregate,
a chocolate turtle on which to choke
while balls bounce horizontally
with natural aim. Kidneys
are the stone-throwers, the delicate
markers embedded in steaks, bringing
forth a futile lymph, a blood
anticorpusculent. Crabs never
have descended until the groceries
like spitfires escape from tents,
from the vegetating scrotum
where cartilage overwhelms
the carefreedom of carpetbaggers
and Newtonian bodies.

CXXXIV

Discus-snakes can slit their throats
from within, swallowing what they
receive where the boomerangs become
shapes of air, retreating in horror
from heat-sensitive glands. Niggardly
globules are fraught with sour cream,
emerging, thieves from a tunnel, from
the tartan pores while writhing bleeders
grind the figures with the tint
of lips. Vestiges of victuals,
they seek a truer career in glens
removed from glamour, in pools
of millenial oils.

CXXXV

Dappled cortisones choose to seethe
where fibrous eggplants bulge
and nestle among the rapeseed, cankerous
zucchini dishing fortitude to what waves.
Winding ways to the robotics dungeons
where links of chrome urge on
the quenching waters, under fireballs
Hebraic cracks shake hands, clapping
and wandering through accelerated
passages meant for invisible items
seen by the holy madmen. Swill
invigorates the rusty corpus, a
straw emerging from his red-smeared
mouth, the sinkhole of a disillusioned mime.
Ginger ale puffs the breasts of
the newsworthy courtesan, and her perfect
marble skin swells a fugitive pink
to firm her lust.

CXXXVI

Dippety doo dah sayeth the savior
under a rented crown of thorns.
Red paint is eaten with tarts,
transmitting the cherry's natural flavor
through the rectum of the earnest ghost,
the luminous thought of pent-up ecstasy
and bloody brains. Towers without mouths
babble; deprived of eyes, they find
their I's, insinuating themselves
into capillaries, cities, great worlds
and the mouths of receptive godsons,
recycling old sputum with acid
and scorning emetics, not to injure
his borrowed loincloth. The corpulent
mysteryman tears his flesh,
having none other.

CXXXVII

Nostrils descend like meaty oars,
windsocks catching gnats, who discover
the dread knocks of gaunt grace,
the dew settling like an appellation,
the blow which is freedom. In the courtyard
the snots confer, half-dried to the
grass, trailing away inside where
they have found refreshments.
Beneath the fleshy spheres
encasing their biscuit party
they make out shouting, a *Lärm*
of grunting and whistling, the passage
of wind through the slaughterhouse.

CXXXVIII

Gaudy cocktails float past the stagelamps,
catching the reflections from beneath
the showgirl's skirt. In the pale venom
of a Scottish spider, the gaunt musculature
of a companion swells, oppressing
the duodenal hydrochloric; beneath his
rustic sweater he reveals unkempt growth
of tangling weeds, a black fastness
upon the kind pillow you'd have
your sleepy, blissful face indent,
drinking a translucent, beneficent ether.
A tiepin's trickle of blood leaves
a hint of molten crayon on the stern flesh;
across the table, he too stirs,
looking shyly with a pent frown
into the clear, reflective pool.
With two stabbing quaffs you both,
in silence and apart like the corners
of the boisterous club, each other
madly mortify, exchanging a cryptic,
hysterically mutual embrace between
your stewing guts while with loud smiles
the girls kick up their heels.

CXXXIX

A masterpiece falls from the wall,
provoking the museum guards. All at once
the stones of prided temples hurl
each other onto the skulls of tourists,
filling the falling smiles of their preservers
with red soup and broken teeth.
The prostrate supplicant yields
the continuity of his spine, and happy
rocks welcome the green overgrowth,
the congregated spores true to the path.
The darkened galleries are full of cloth,
old canvasses on cracked stretchers,
torn to shreds by the rageful rampageous
busts, the age-old marbles who trumpet
holy demands to clouds serene and blasting,
to creative craftsmen unmoved by their art.

CXL

A helmet passed from skull to skull,
as they measured surrogate opiums,
draughts of dispersed creosote.
Sense like a mule fell from the womb,
limply drained, shorn of coherent
appearance. Licking dry stamps,
the old woman crossed her legs,
nursing with felt a stitched
course, a weary robot like
golems dancing with broomsticks.
Pens coagulated, seeking caps.
Ah, the uniforms, filled out
by groups of men! The posted
raptures flew, transported
by sullen missionaries, to
distant daughters sluggishly
contemplating divorces.

CXLI

Gringos, wogs, spics, kikes, and the eloquent
farmer in colloquy scrambled the oats, dishing
fish to fogged semblances, betokened closets
courted by gits. Himself the hip towed
the slope, ghosting paraphrases, hosting
towels entranced by membranes. Be roped
naughty knacks, finished foment volatile
viands. Caskets disc fondle soaped roasts
angelically bones. Beaued chord simple
Xavier established penumbras. Pish.
Solely nuggets? Foughty dish-ish foreigns
receiving soggy cream and bruised peaches.

CXLII

To loose the ladders, tracking nasturtiums
into the gristle of gospels, is the disavowal
of angels, the crunch of disconcerted mandibles
shorn from pale blue tresses, swinging hammocks
obscured by foaming bees. Depilatory agents
produce their holsters, waving harmonic ropes
inelastic; the bugs are shaved, and the
starksome faeries, plunging beneath cubed
foreheads and desolate umbrellas, suspended
by the indifferent bubbles like solemnly
placed advertisements at the same location
since ___, trail their hands behind the wind,
still clutching treacherous rungs
and shreds of webbed wisps. They traffic
through a lightless brink, tracing
a neon arrow between invisible fates.

CXLIII

Asps lick the marble bust, which eyes
them without repugnance. Crowned
by speckled bands, the Caesar is silent,
a stony potentate unmarked by pupils.
Quoits descend like thorns, as
the fun-loving schoolchildren playfully adorn
the smooches of a mistress, the acetic
sponge of a martyred maniac. Even you,
with brutal thrusts, mold the quiet
kings, the serene reflectors splotching
the sides of marble chambers, who
turn over careers from the frozen wilds
to the tumult of your fantasy.

CXLIV

Sidereal gourds notch the geese, who
collapse in dejection. Sorties
of whispers wear hats as they progress
beneath the bushes, rustling
and plowing the soil with
eager patience. In hospitals
they don turbans, wrapping their
torsos with shredded pink sheets,
dousing the nurses with frantic fingernail,
shrapnel of their identities.

Index of First Lines

A

A belt of cutting crystal lies 85
A buzz like a white sheet 114
A cat, sprung from Deutschland 121
A corridor, humid with the panting 79
A crumbling binding upon a hill startles 21
A crystal glass of sputum 14
A dearth of overhanging toruses or spindles 68
A gasp, a gurgle through the clogged gelatine 131
A helmet passed from skull to skull 140
A high harness rests on the hillside 23
A horde approached, carrying 43
A masterpiece falls from the wall 139
A midget iguana crawls back to sea 15
A practising surgeon, his glasses affixed to a whiskified Polaris 45
A ripe jug of gilded flies 71
A solar concentration inhabits my kitchen 3
A soul is laid out for stew, configured 24
A sublime crusade is planned for pilgrims, a surefooted 99
A substantial plasma, self-reflecting 97
A subversion of grasses spills wine 120
A vast chart hangs from a purple clotted cloud 20

An acid swarms on the floor, grinning. 69
An origin is filth aground, a turd 6
Anxious dogs flick the outcast cans 106
Asps lick the marble bust, which eyes 143
At maximum carrot peelings, at the most 53
At the secret signal the lizard-skinned forearm. 25

B

Behind the curtain of red steam, if. 61
Beneath the rapids in suspension 16
Between sheaths of sightless grasses 12

C

Claws of lobsters form ridges 95
Curled horns of amber 'fore 8
Cutlets provide the hostelry for green molds 72

D

Dappled cortisones choose to seethe 135
Daughters sense the necks of minions. 107
Dealing with gaunt, spoken wits 86
Death is in squirrels or encased in what 27
Decent members at the spittoons. 109
Digging a wet hole in the mold 62
Dimly licks assault the inkwell, grinning 91
Dippety doo dah sayeth the savior. 136
Discus-snakes can slit their throats 134
Dishtowels, smoking a fibrous batch of green larvae 112
Disregarded hoots resound in the mist 101
Dissident hazes engulf roving vermin 67
Dorsal fins are found afloat. 103
Dribble. Whatsoever unceasingly. 1

Dried Zoroastrians cry aloud to the sandwich-maker............48
Drinking lemonade, the forests give........................81

F

Fertile imps fret over turnips, counting....................75
Fibbed snorters cower now................................115
Fidgeting with overgrown moats, broken....................80
Fipply nisps fint the dampers..............................89
Fists cannot clap, and the robbers........................132
Forgotten physicists fondle babes.........................123
Fortuitous morticians spit out gristly tears................70
Forty are arranged. In cupboardlike........................58
Frigged eyes point outwards...............................55
Froh-ed Horace is the pastoral wench....................65
From his vest at the bus-stop.............................125
Frozen green forces imbibe their livery....................44
Frozen ozones greet their wimps..........................104
Full of the granulate force of his grinder..................63

G

Gaping at the filtered star, natives........................94
Gaskets blaze a rancid fume..............................108
Gaudy cocktails float past the stagelamps.................138
Greasing the fender, the youth turns around...............110
Greasy Bobby fits the bill, smelling........................90
Greeted by the headlights at gloaming......................74
Greeting the hilarity of the gorgon.........................54
Gringos, wogs, spics, kikes, and the eloquent.............141
Gripping figged masses, the head bears down..............83
Gummed labels of another year............................32
Gyped envoys fork the harpooned kites....................84

H

Heady wombs approach the ravine 17
Hideous! The blossoms 10
Hydra like florid dwarves. 42

I

I am presented upon the occasion 73
I cannot relate what feeds upon bodies 34
In the garden where feckless resins. 29
In the wok sounds a bell 130

J

Jelly and ritual; the syllable 13

K

Kaspar, inspecting an apple, deems it *klug* 98

L

Like a bratsome wok, splitting. 113
Like a green path of air 33
Like a gross formula embedded in 59
Like a particolored rope his mind wheedles its length 87
Like Robert to engage the arms of an octopus. 39
Lotus crap drips grease onto the snozzled. 100

M

Many codfish coerced the hound, tearing. 82
Men bent at gloaming over their sandwiches 9
Mystery fowl alight upon. 2

N

Naughty fibs cannot sort their whites 92
Noodles strung in shit reach 30
Nostrils descend like meaty oars 137

P

Persistent turd, where three-legged 40
Portentous, unread Talmud, on the high 7
Pustules like wire fret their tongs 88

Q

Quiescent rivers enlarge their troughs 56

R

Rescinded like a man crossing the street 37
Robert sucks diamonds for retreating whores 46
Robert, knowing snozzles, grins at artichokes 41
Rolling dander incinerates the court 127

S

Seated frogs introduce smoke 66
Seven deaths walk the streets 47
Seven doorknobs are confounded, and knocks 78
Short-haired, among the cilia which and cilia 77
Sidereal gourds notch the geese, who 144
Silent forests respect mosses 57
Sinking into the white porcelain quagmire 118
Slyly hugging the enclosure, Robert returns 116
Spatulas snicker behind the fronds 126
Squalidly waiting, dangling from a seated finger 124

Steamed rotors nudge the naughty nuggets 105
Stormy dungeons rape the oarlocks 60
Sun-candles unfixed, in swarms 11

T

The bout, like diffident brands 96
The cat sleeps, while rubber burns 128
The color of scissors, scissors who 22
The corner of the mouth 5
The doctor's visor casts a shadow 50
The glare of twenty-six preens in inverse proportion 18
The mustachioed Deutscher peels away leaves 129
The nuisance is an aggregate 133
The prize is a hot towel, a 38
The sun busies himself with another quarter 35
The sun on the grass kneads forth prudish lumps 26
The sun threatens my house, claiming 31
The tinned sardine is a headless whore 19
The tortoise rigorously proceeds a step 111
There is a green dust of this planet 4
To loose the ladders, tracking nasturtiums 142
Tonight the moon is a polite reflective platter 117
Torrid waists are encircled 49
Tusked mailmen ride to work, hanging 93

U

Under the dark city the tunnel runs 119
Under the horizon there swoops a great bird 52

W

Warped bridges sort their toiletries 64
Whips lie clear on lutulent sagas 122

White, grey, and green, the mucus of 28
Wimped digits flick their fronds 76
With blood goes pallidly 102
Without wings the runner 36

Y

Your mouth drops a thread 51